W9-BRX-654

Jinxed

TRUE STORIES ★

BASEBALL
SUPERSTITIONS
FROM AROUND THE
MAJOR LEAGUES

Edited by Ken Leiker

Ballantine Books
New York

Published in the United States by Ballantine Books, an imprint of The Random House Publishing Group, a division of Random House, Inc., New York.

BALLANTINE and colophon are registered trademarks of Random House, Inc.

ISBN 0-345-48544-0

Printed in the United States of America on acid-free paper

www.ballantinebooks.com

9 8 7 6 5 4 3 2 1

First Edition

Designed by Rare Air Media

Acknowledgments

Some things never go out of style, no matter how different the world looks. To put this book together, we called on longtime friends who are among the best in the country at what they do. Bob Elliott, Jack Etkin, Paul Hagen, Scott Miller and Bob Nightengale have more than 100 years of combined experience covering Major League Baseball. In a game that marches relentlessly from early spring to late fall, they remain pros who have kept a lively pace. More than that, they are our friends, and their work can be found throughout this book.

Alyson Footer, Mike Berardino and Hal McCoy, as well, are highly respected baseball writers who enthusiastically answered our call for tales of the superstitious and, in some cases, downright weird characters that add texture to the game.

At Rare Air Media, the talented Nick DeCarlo created a design for *Jinxed* that masterfully complements the text while maintaining the poise and professionalism we have come to expect from him, despite the strain of long hours and tight deadlines.

At Ballantine Books, special thanks goes to Jennifer Osborne for her kind words and encouragement. And as always, Anthony Ziccardi, Bill Takes and Gina Centrello lent their expertise and support all along the way.

—*Ken Leiker and Mark Vancil*
May 2005

the *Players*

Introduction

Nothing in the world of sports and entertainment compares to the rhythm of a professional baseball season. There is no clock, play list, script or time slot. The game rolls along at its own pace through spring, summer and fall, ending just short of winter. Appropriately for a game that isn't over until the last out is made, success in baseball is measured in terms of failure.

Combine the long roll of a season with the constant buzz of failure, and it is no wonder that a player's search for divine guidance, if not intervention, knows no bounds, even among the best of players. Ken Griffey Jr. sold his car because every time he drove it to a game he failed to get a hit. What seemed obvious to Griffey, "The car had no hits in it," might suggest something else for those outside the lines.

St. Louis Cardinals manager Tony La Russa sometimes prints the names on his lineup card and other times writes in cursive. His pattern? Simple. If he prints and the team wins, he continues to print until they lose. Only then does he switch to cursive.

Larry Walker does virtually everything in a multiple of three, all in the name of good luck. How seriously does Mr. Walker take his commitment to the number three? His ex-wife got $3 million in their divorce settlement.

Jinxed relates the attempt by baseball players to put order into a game that often appears to have none. Why does a line drive drop in front of an outfielder one day, and sail directly into his glove the next? Is it just a game of inches, or are there metaphysical forces at play? No one knows, but most players look for evidence of the latter and act accordingly.

Jinxed is a compilation of the often strange but true routines carried out by ballplayers, managers and coaches to keep themselves on the right side of whatever god favors base hits over lazy fly balls, and pitches that catch the corners over those that just miss.

Compiled by editor Ken Leiker and baseball writers Bob Nightengale, Paul Hagen, Jack Etkin, Scott Miller, Alyson Footer, Hal McCoy, Mike Berardino and Bob Elliott, *Jinxed* is about paying attention to detail in a season based on survival.

It's about hope.

It's baseball.

Joe McEwing

When Joe McEwing is playing third or second base, he'll run onto the field and touch that particular base at the start of every inning. McEwing always touches the base the same way: left foot right foot and a hop on the base with the left foot.

"It's a reminder to stay focused and be ready," said McEwing, who entered his eighth major league season in 2005. Playing for the St. Louis Cardinals, New York Mets and Kansas City Royals, he had appeared at every position except pitcher and catcher in his career.

Between pitches, McEwing has a set routine, one that might be described as fidgety or animated. He'll step out of the box and take a deep breath and swing, all the while "reminding myself to stay focused and clear my mind from what just happened on that previous pitch," he said.

"Get everything completely out of my mind before I step back in."

McEwing hops as he takes his practice swings. He used to be more animated as he would ready himself for the next pitch, but he has "calmed down" his routine in recent years.

Why?

"Getting a few letters from the league about staying out of the box too long," McEwing said. "I take my time, but compared to a normal guy's time, it's probably the same. It's just that I moved around more."

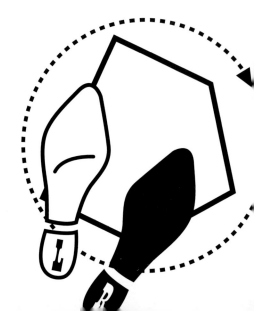

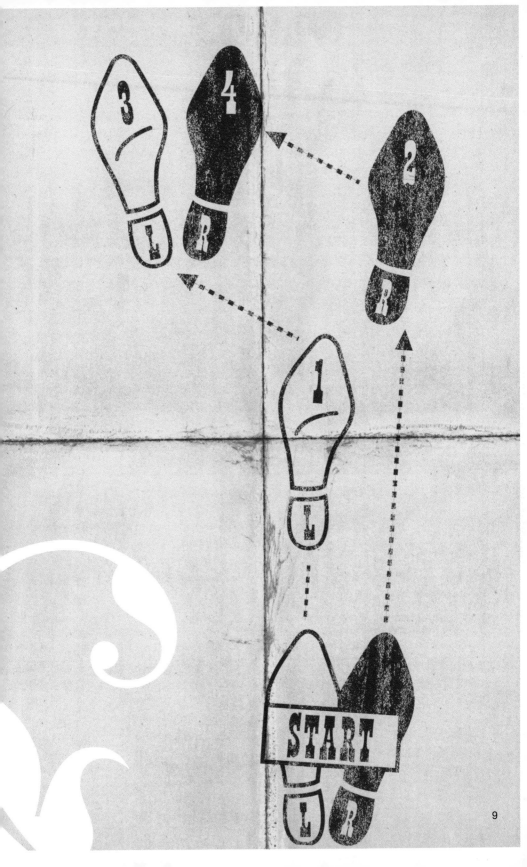

9

Doug Mientkiewicz

Candy, fast food and crystals are key elements in keeping New York Mets first baseman Doug Mientkiewicz at the top of his game. Does that sound like a lot of work? It is. But Mientkiewicz has a loving wife and a doting mother who eagerly indulge his many superstitions.

If Mientkiewicz is hitting well, it's likely because he's been frequenting his favorite fast food restaurant. "Sometimes we'll have to eat at McDonald's two or three days in a row," says his wife, Jodi Mientkiewicz. "It sounds terrible, because it's not the most healthy thing. But McDonald's has hits in it."

So do gummy bears, licorice and Tootsie Pops. Mientkiewicz has snacked on gummy bears before going to bed, certain they would bring him good luck. His mother, on the other hand, believes that licorice and Tootsie Pops are the key to a .300 batting average. She is often among the crowd at his games, doling out the sweet treats to those seated near her when her son gets a hit, hopeful of keeping his luck going.

Mother Mientkiewicz doesn't rely on just candy. She also dresses for the occasion, wearing clothing that she had on at previous games when Doug hit well.

On the field, Mientkiewicz sometimes will dash into the clubhouse between innings and change shoes. That ritual was born when he fell into a 5-for-110 slump at the outset of a minor league season in New Britain, Connecticut. The New Britain batter's box would get softer as the game progressed, Mientkiewicz said, so he changed shoes one night and dropped in a hit. He continued the shoe-change practice and emerged from his slump, and ever since then he's been lacing up so often that he might as well be working at Foot Locker.

Crystals also became an integral part of Mientkiewicz's repertoire at New Britain. One day Jodi purchased a couple of pebble-sized pieces of crystal and gave one to Doug. He placed them in his locker, and she held onto hers while sitting in the stands. Doug went on a hitting tear and won the Eastern League batting title in 1998 with a .323 average.

The following year, Mientkiewicz went to spring training with the Minnesota Twins in Fort Myers, Florida, as the leading candidate to become the team's regular first baseman. But he didn't hit well in the early Grapefruit League games, and panic began to set in. That's when Doug and Jodi realized they had forgotten to bring their lucky crystal pieces with them.

Jodi set out for a store in Fort Myers that carried crystals. "I saw a lot of crystals, but no amethyst," she said, referring to the purple variety of quartz that she had originally purchased. "I asked if they had any, and the lady said no."

Jodi would not—could not—accept that answer. She peeked into several drawers behind the counter, and one was filled with amethyst crystals. Jodi scooped up a handful, threw down her money and dashed out. "My wife almost got arrested in that store," Mientkiewicz said with a sly grin.

Instead, she had a handful of good luck when she arrived at the ballpark. "I got to the field, holding it in my hand, and Doug hit a home run in his first at-bat," Jodi said. He went 2-for-4 that day, performed well the rest of the spring and earned a job with the Twins.

Brendan Donnelly

After suffering a broken nose while shagging fly balls in the outfield during spring training in 2004, Los Angeles Angels relief pitcher Brendan Donnelly was careful to avoid another setback in 2005. Not that he would admit to intentionally altering his spring training regimen in Tempe, Arizona. Much of the change, he claimed, was coincidental.

"I happened to have a different room," Donnelly said. "I happened to go with a baggier uniform. I happened to take a different route to the ballpark."

Donnelly, though, readily acknowledges that he has superstitions and indulges them at the ballpark. "I have a lot of them," he said. "Mine pretty much start at 1 P.M."

About 30 minutes before every game, Donnelly eats a toasted peanut butter and jelly sandwich. He started doing it in the minor leagues, where clubhouse cuisine is limited. "We didn't have real food in the minor leagues," he said. "That's what they gave you: peanut butter and jelly. The pregame spread was PBJ—toasted, if you wanted to get fancy."

Donnelly goes to the bullpen when the game starts, but always returns to the clubhouse in the third inning to limber up. He returns to the bullpen in the fifth inning. "There are some things I do in the clubhouse that aren't going to be talked about," he said cryptically.

His routines are tried and true, Donnelly said, and he wouldn't think of not following them faithfully.

"You could say all this doesn't do anything for me," he said. "It's routine. Baseball is routine. You throw at the same time, you stretch at a certain time before the game, you do certain things in the bullpen. It's all about preparation. I'm a routine guy."

Lenny Dykstra

Lenny Dykstra, a three-time All-Star center fielder with the Philadelphia Phillies in the 1990s, could practically keep a sporting goods company in business all by himself. Before each game he would line up six sets of batting gloves. Not just any gloves. These were high-end items made of extra-soft leather.

"One new set for batting practice and five for the game," said John Vukovich, a teammate of Dykstra's. "If he got a single his first time up, he'd wear that pair for the rest of the game. But if he hit a line drive for an out, they'd go into the garbage can, and he'd have a new set for his second at-bat."

Dykstra was just as fussy about his uniform. If he didn't get a hit in his first two at-bats, he would go to the clubhouse for a complete change — jersey, pants, socks, underwear, everything. If he got a hit early, though, he would stick with the same apparel for the whole game, no matter how grass- or dirt-stained it became.

Getting hits wasn't the sole focus of Dykstra's superstitions. If the Phillies won the previous game, he would make certain to play catch with the same teammate during pregame warm-up the following day.

If they lost, he would find a new partner.

A beneficiary of Dykstra's quirks was Vukovich's son, Vince, who was then a high school baseball player in South Jersey. He went on to play at the University of Delaware, and was drafted and signed by the Phillies. Whenever Dykstra would discard a pair of practically new batting gloves, John Vukovich would retrieve them from the trash and give them to his son. "My kid had more new batting gloves than any kid in America," Vukovich said.

Earl Weaver

Earl Weaver was selected to the baseball Hall of Fame for his achievement as the Baltimore Orioles manager from 1968 to 1986. Brilliant and innovative as he was, he wasn't above engaging in superstition, as well.

Like most mortals, Weaver put on his pants one leg at a time. But when he was pulling on his baseball pants, it had to be the left leg first. If he inadvertently led with his right leg, he instinctively started over.

Weaver had many nervous habits in the dugout. One of them involved thread.

"He'd tell [pitching coach] George Bamberger to get him a piece of thread, and Earl would wrap it around his fingers for luck," said Elrod Hendricks, a catcher on many of Weaver's teams. "If we weren't scoring runs, he'd look for it."

In the manner of Madame Defarge and her knitting in *A Tale of Two Cities*, Weaver would sit in the dugout and attempt to manipulate the game's outcome with his piece of thread. Back and forth he would move the thread, which was wrapped around both of his index fingers.

While thread was a key piece of equipment for Weaver, he never seemed to carry any with him. Someone always had to find it for him.

"One day Bamberger didn't have it," Hendricks said. "Earl said, 'What the hell

do you mean? You're going to find some thread.' He didn't care what kind it was. He just needed some thread."

Bamberger scurried back to the clubhouse and conducted an exhaustive search until he found a piece of string that would pacify his boss. Bamberger undoubtedly is the only pitching coach in major league history whose duties included thread patrol.

Weaver also smoked cigarettes to calm himself, rarely getting through a game without indulging his nicotine addiction. He would duck into the runway leading to the clubhouse and fire up a butt.

"Earl would smoke at any time. He'd smoke more when Don Stanhouse came in the game," said Hendricks, referring to an Orioles' relief pitcher who was successful but rarely retired the side in order. "That was survival. That was prayer."

Back and forth he would move the thread, which was wrapped around both of his index fingers.

Curt Schilling

Curt Schilling has pitched in enough games on national television that most baseball fans know he always makes a point of skipping over the foul line on his way to the mound and when he returns to the dugout.

His most personal ritual, though, is leaving a ticket for his late father for every game that he starts. Cliff Schilling died of a heart attack in 1988.

Curt was a U.S. Army brat who was born in Alaska and moved frequently as a kid. The day he came home from the hospital after his birth, his father placed a baseball and glove in his crib.

Cliff Schilling grew up in the coal mining country of western Pennsylvania and was a passionate fan of the Pittsburgh Pirates and Pittsburgh Steelers. His favorite player was Roberto Clemente. The first major league game Curt attended was at Pittsburgh's Three Rivers Stadium on September 30, 1972, the last day of the regular season. Curt saw Clemente get his 3,000th hit, which would be his last. Clemente died three months later in an airplane crash.

Cliff had a profound effect on his son's early baseball career. In high school in Phoenix, Arizona, Curt had a difference of opinion with the baseball coach, and he wasn't the only one. Some of the more influential families in the school district circulated a petition to have the coach fired after their sons didn't make the team.

Cliff wouldn't support the petition, even though Curt had problems with the coach. "My dad told me I would play for men I didn't agree with," Curt said. "Some I wouldn't like, and my options were to shut up and play, or quit. I was always taught never to speak back to an umpire or a coach.

"That was a valuable lesson. I learned that no matter what you think is fair in life, sometimes others see things differently. Whether it was fair or not that I didn't play varsity until my senior year was beside the point."

The first time Curt's father saw him

pitch professionally was after Curt had been named to the South Atlantic League All-Star team and had been voted the league's player of the month. Cliff accepted the award on Curt's behalf, then Curt took the mound and didn't pitch well enough to make it through the second inning. "But I knew he was proud of me," Curt said.

When Cliff died, his son lost a father, friend and confidant. The two had talked at least once a week during the season since Curt had left home in 1986 to begin his professional career. Cliff had a calming

and reassuring influence on his high-strung son. Unfortunately, the father died several months before his son made it to the major leagues.

Curt developed into one of the best pitchers in the major leagues, became an integral part of two World Series championship teams, the co-MVP of the 2001 Series, but he never forgot the lessons his father taught him. Every time he is scheduled to pitch, Curt leaves a ticket for his father, who is absent from his son's life only in the flesh.

Scott Eyre

San Francisco Giants relief pitcher Scott Eyre admits to many superstitions, and readily acknowledges that most of them have come from his teammates over the years.

"My chair at my locker has to be facing toward the door of the clubhouse," Eyre said. "When it's moved, boy, do I get mad." He stole that one from Albert Belle when they both played for the Chicago White Sox in 1997 and 1998.

Eyre always requests a uniform number that adds up to 11. "Manny Mota was my favorite player when I was growing up. I have to honor him," said Eyre, who has number 47 on his Giants jersey.

Eyre walks to the bullpen after the Giants have batted in the first inning—never before. "A few guys did that in Toronto," said Eyre, who played for the Blue Jays in 2001 and 2002, "and it just seemed like the cool thing to do."

He never goes to the bullpen without a Diet Coke in hand. "I stole that one from Dan Plesac," said Eyre, who played with Plesac in Toronto. "I have to have it with me. I don't even drink it. It just sits there. But when somebody else takes a sip of it or drinks all of it, I get pissed."

Even though he doesn't drink the soda, Eyre wouldn't think of carrying any brand with him except Diet Coke. "I just know it works," he said with conviction. "One day in Toronto I was late getting dressed and didn't take it to the bullpen with me. "You know what happened? I got lit up. That's the last time I'll do something stupid like that."

Jason Johnson

Detroit Tigers third base coach Juan Samuel was standing in the dugout before a game. A fan in the stands caught his attention, asking for a baseball. Samuel obliged. He saw a ball sitting on the bench, picked it up and flipped it to the fan. And then all hell broke loose.

Pitching coach Bob Cluck began frantically searching for another baseball. Someone else yelled that they had to make sure right-hander Jason Johnson, the Tigers' starting pitcher that night, hadn't noticed what happened.

After finishing his warm-up session in the bullpen, Johnson always takes the last baseball he threw and brings it to the dugout with him and places it carefully on the back of the bench. No one is supposed to touch it.

It wasn't the first time Samuel had noticed that Johnson was a little different. On another occasion, game time was fast approaching, and Samuel noticed that Johnson had not begun warming up yet.

When Samuel asked about it, he was told not to worry, that Johnson always appeared precisely at 44 minutes past the hour. Sure enough, no sooner had the scoreboard clock clicked to double fours that Johnson appeared in the dugout and headed for the bullpen.

"Pitchers—they're all crazy," said Samuel, an All-Star second baseman in three of his 16 major league seasons.

Jim Thome

Entering the 2005 season, Philadelphia Phillies first baseman Jim Thome had gone to bat more than 7,000 times and hit 423 home runs in the major leagues. Each time he extended his right arm—Thome is a left-handed batter—and pointed his bat at the pitcher after settling into his stance. It had become as much Thome's trademark as wearing his stirrup socks high.

Thome's bat-pointing routine began when he was playing in the minor leagues in 1993 at Charlotte, North Carolina, a Triple-A team. Manager Charlie Manuel was seeking a method to help Thome relax when he was batting.

Manuel got his inspiration from an unlikely source: the actor Robert Redford.

Thome had made brief appearances in the major leagues with the Cleveland Indians in 1991 and 1992, but he didn't hit well enough to stay. Manuel believed that Thome was too tense at the plate, and thus unable to take full advantage of his powerful swing.

Manuel discussed Thome's problem with his coaches, Luis Isaac and Dyar Miller, on a bus trip from Pawtucket,

Rhode Island, to Scranton, Pennsylvania. None of the men had any ideas that might help Thome. When the bus arrived at Lackawanna County Stadium, Manuel walked into the visiting team's clubhouse and glanced at the television set. The movie *The Natural* happened to be playing.

"It was the part where Roy Hobbs [the character played by Redford] points his bat toward the pitcher. And it just hit me," said Manuel, who became the Phillies' manager in 2005.

"Jim had gone something like 106 or 116 at-bats without hitting a ball to the right of second base. He had been to the big leagues and it was something that was talked about, how he seemed to be late on pitches and hit everything over the third base dugout."

Manuel took Thome to the batting cage. He told him that as he settled into his stance, he wanted him to point his bat at the pitcher and take a deep breath. He also told Thome to open his stance slightly.

Thome was reluctant to point his bat, fearing that it would appear as if he was showing up the pitcher, but he agreed to give it a try. That night against a left-handed pitcher, he hit a home run to right center field in his first at-bat. Next he cracked a double down the right field line. Later Thome pulled a pitch for another hit.

A star was born that night. Maybe they'll make a movie about him someday.

"Jim had gone something like 106 or 116 at-bats without hitting a ball to the right of second base."

Steve Kline

Baltimore Orioles relief pitcher Steve Kline needs more time than most to ready himself for a game. It's a wonder that he doesn't wear himself out before he gets on the mound.

"I've got to wear the same hat, and wear the same socks that are marked L and R so I know which one goes on which foot," Kline says. "I've got to wear the same shorts, the same jock, the same shirt that I wear for every game. I have to wear the same things for batting practice every day."

Once the game starts, Kline is back and forth between the clubhouse and the field until the late innings. He knows that he won't pitch until then.

"In the first inning, I have a song that I go into the weight room and listen to," he said. "I come in and drink something in the fifth inning. In the sixth, I go in and put water on my face to get myself ready to go. And then I pace until I get in the game."

Kline joined the Orioles in 2005 after serving the previous four seasons as the St. Louis Cardinals' primary left-handed reliever. He believes that his rituals prepare him for success.

"I'm really big on superstitions," Kline said. "If I don't do that stuff, I feel as if I didn't do something that day."

1ST INNING

5TH INNING

Wade Boggs

Wade Boggs, who became a member of the baseball Hall of Fame in 2005, ate chicken every day of his 18-year major league career. The fowl diet probably wasn't responsible for any of Boggs' 3,010 hits, but as the years rolled on and the hits kept coming, he didn't dare change his dining habit.

It began as a financial matter. Chicken is cheaper than beef, and Boggs had limited meal money during his five-plus years in the minor leagues. By the time he reached the major leagues in 1982, chicken was no longer an option—it was a ritual. His wife, Debbie, had 52 recipes for preparing chicken, all included in *Fowl Tips,* the cookbook she authored.

"Anybody who can cook chicken every day for 18 years deserves the Nobel Peace Prize," Boggs said in tribute to his wife.

Boggs' eccentric behavior wasn't limited to his diet. The chicken-eating man followed a precise schedule, too. He left for the ballpark each day at 1:47, and ran pregame sprints at 7:17 before a night game. The number 7 was significant to him because he aspired for a 7-for-7 game—seven hits in as many at-bats, a feat accomplished only twice in major league history.

Each time he went to the plate, Boggs used his bat to sketch into the batter's box dirt what he believed to be a "7" with a line through it. "It started when I was in Little League," he said. "I saw it in a magazine, and it said it brought good luck. So I wrote it in the dirt to wish myself luck before I got into the batter's box.

"I didn't find out until 1984 it was a religious insignia."

What Boggs had seen in the magazine and was scratching into the dirt was the Hebrew *chai* symbol. *Chai* means "life."

Boggs also engaged in rituals at third base, his regular position. He raced to his spot for the start of a home game the moment the grounds crew finished watering the infield dirt, before any other players got to their position. Once there, he searched the ground for three rocks or pebbles and tossed them off the field.

After the game, Boggs insisted on the same meal: two hot dogs, a bag of Lay's barbecue potato chips and a glass of iced tea.

Former Los Angeles Angels manager Gene Mauch once attempted to disrupt Boggs' ritualistic behavior. Mauch had a technician freeze the Anaheim Stadium scoreboard clock for five minutes when it reached 7:15. Boggs was doing stretching exercises in preparation for his sprints, glancing occasionally at the clock. Soon his glance became a confused stare, much to the amusement of Mauch and the Angels players. Finally, the scoreboard clock turned to 7:20.

"Since I never remember seeing Boggs go hitless against us, I figure he probably got his two or three hits anyway," Mauch said years later.

Did Boggs really believe that his rituals could make him a better player? In a word, yes.

"Basically all superstitions are a form of mind relaxation," he said. "They distract you from the day-to-day grind and make the day flow that much easier."

Who's to argue? Boggs batted .328 for his career, and five of his season averages were higher than .350.

"You hit like Wade Boggs did," said St. Louis Cardinals manager Tony La Russa, "and I wouldn't change anything either."

> **"Anybody who can cook chicken every day for 18 years deserves the Nobel Peace Prize."**

Jim Lefebvre

As a player, coach and manager in the major leagues, Jim Lefebvre engaged in what some would call eccentric behavior, although he considered it to be progressive thinking.

One of Lefebvre's innovations as a hitting coach was to use pink softballs instead of regular baseballs for specialized drills to sharpen a batter's visual skills. He later endorsed a ball that featured four colored panels. The batter was instructed to call out the color upon making contact, a drill designed to develop focus and concentration.

Lefebvre's goal when he became manager of the Seattle Mariners in 1989 was a winning season, a feat that the team would achieve for the first time in 1991, in its 15th year of existence. During his three years as manager, Lefebvre was always quick to do whatever he could to change the Mariners' fortunes.

For reasons known only to himself, Lefebvre was wearing pink leopard-pattern compression tights under his uniform one day. The Mariners won, so the manager wore the same tights the next day. They continued to win, mounting a rare streak of success, and Lefebvre continued to wear his lucky pink tights. The players apparently were more amused than inspired. "You could see them under his white baseball pants," said center fielder Ken Griffey Jr.

On another occasion, the Mariners won several home games in a row, and Lefebvre noted that he had sat on the same dugout cushion throughout the success. He ordered the team's equipment manager to pack the cushion for the coming road trip. Unfortunately, the cushion had run out of wins.

Larry Andersen

Longtime relief pitcher Larry Andersen always looked at things a bit differently—his keen sense of humor was the tip-off to that. But have you ever heard of a baseball player who was too superstitious to use smokeless tobacco?

"I wouldn't dip when I pitched," said Andersen, who worked in 699 games for six teams in a 17-year major league career that ended in 1994. "I was dipping at one time, but it got into me that I couldn't do it anymore when I was pitching. It was a superstition. I don't know how it started, or where."

Instead, Andersen chewed gum. And, yep, as you probably guessed . . . "If I had a good inning, I'd leave the gum in," he said. "If I had a bad inning, I'd spit it out and get another piece."

Dwight Gooden was superstitious with his gum, too. But at least he didn't bring barbers into his ritualistic behavior.

"One thing that always concerned me was getting a haircut," Andersen said. "If I was going good, I didn't want to get a hair-cut. If I was going bad, I'd go get a haircut." Which led to an age-old debate more than once: success, or vanity?

"If I got to the point where I needed a haircut but I was going good, I thought about it," Andersen said.

It never got to the point that Andersen felt he gained strength from his hair, in the manner of Hall of Fame relief pitcher Dennis Eckersley and his famous locks. "I never got to Eck's length," Andersen said. "I don't think I could grow that much hair, anyway."

No doubt, a bad-hair day is among the countless excuses that major league players have privately cited for failing to perform adequately. "There are so many things," Andersen said, "you can almost talk yourself into having a bad game."

33

Ray King

Relief pitcher Ray King always wears the same T-shirt under his St. Louis Cardinals uniform. On the front of the shirt is Mr. Happy Crack, a smiling concrete block with a crack running through it, and the words: A dry crack is a happy crack.

On the back is the name of the business: The Crack Team. Foundation Repair Specialists.

King said he and his wife were driving in St. Louis in 2004 and saw a truck with a smiling, cracked concrete block on the side. King said he began joking about it, and the following day—much to his disbelief, because he had never met anyone from the business—King found a box at his locker containing Happy Crack T-shirts.

King considered the 2004 season to be the best of his career. His accomplishments while wearing a Happy Crack T-shirt included pitching 21 consecutive scoreless innings over 30 appearances. But when the Cardinals played in Los Angeles in the National League Division Series, the shirt was lost in the laundry.

In St. Louis' 10-7 win against Houston in Game 1 of the NL Championship Series, King yielded a home run to Lance Berkman. In postgame interviews, the good-natured King, not to make excuses, mentioned that he'd lost his lucky T-shirt.

Someone with The Crack Team must have heard about King's plight on the news that night, because the next day King found a box with about three dozen T-shirts at his locker. King gave up another home run to Berkman during the series, but he also made two scoreless appearances. And in three games against Boston in the World Series, he pitched 2⅔ scoreless innings.

"When I packed for spring training," King said, "I made sure my Happy Crack T-shirt was there. Call it superstition or not, but I'm going to keep wearing it."

When he pulls on his lucky T-shirt, King almost always is in a good mood, a state he achieves by listening to the same CD, a Kenny G jazz collection, on his way to the ballpark. "If I'm at home, it's in my car," King said. "If I'm on the road, it's on my iPod. Got to have that, because no matter what went on that day, no matter

A DRY CRACK IS A HAPPY CRACK

how hectic it was or how great, it always puts me in a zone where I'm mellowing out going to the ballpark."

King was pitching for the Milwaukee Brewers when he bought the CD in a Minneapolis mall. "You know how you can sample CDs?" King said. "The next thing I knew I'd been standing there for, like, 30 minutes. It was soothing. I bought it, and it's been with me ever since."

_id Eckstein _
_arry Walker R
_lbert Pujols 1
Scott Rolen 3B
Jim Edmonds
Reggie Sander_
_ Mark Grudzi_
_ Yadier Molin_

Tony La Russa

St. Louis Cardinals manager Tony La Russa sometimes prints the names on his lineup card and other times writes in cursive. What's his pattern? Simple. If he prints and the team wins, he continues to print until they lose. Only then does he switch to cursive.

La Russa admits to having many superstitions but is reluctant to reveal them, fearing a self-inflicted hex. He did reach into his managerial past with the Chicago White Sox in 1982 for one superstitious tale.

"There was a death threat against me, so I had to wear a bulletproof vest for a weekend series," La Russa said. "I wore a jacket over the vest, and we won the series, so I kept the jacket on. We won 15 out of 18, and I kept wearing that jacket.

"We were playing Texas at Texas, and I went home for the birth of my daughter Devon. I was watching the game on TV. We had fallen behind. Ken Silvestri was our pitching coach. All of a sudden I look, and somebody had gone into the club-house and brought a jacket out.

"Silvestri had my jacket on, and we rallied to tie the game in the ninth. Dennis Lamp gave up a hit to lose the game for us in the 11th. But they had gone into the clubhouse to get my stupid jacket."

La Russa was the Cardinals manager when the team played a game in Milwaukee and both teams wore 1982 replica uniforms. (St. Louis beat the Brewers in the 1982 World Series.) For the Cardinals, that meant powder blue, belt-less uniforms, the baseball style in an era of polyester and double-knit fashions.

Before the game, La Russa told equipment manager Buddy Bates, "If we win today, we're wearing these frickin' uniforms tomorrow." That, of course, would not have been allowed, and it became a moot point when the Cardinals lost.

Lou Skizas

Lou Skizas was a bit player in the major leagues, getting into 239 games with four teams from 1956 to 1959. He hit 18 home runs for the Kansas City Athletics in 1957, but his greatest claim to fame was his nickname—"The Nervous Greek"—and a batting ritual that has yet to be copied.

Skizas batted right-handed. As he settled into the batter's box and readied himself for a pitch, he would thrust his right hand into the back pocket of his pants and take practice swings using only his left arm. As the pitcher went into his motion, Skizas would pull his right hand out of his pocket and place it on the bat.

He repeated the ritual for every pitch. What was in his back pocket? Skizas, a devout follower of the Greek Orthodox religion, always carried a large crucifix symbolic of his faith, and he constantly touched it for good luck.

Should he ever doubt the power of the crucifix, Skizas sometimes was served with a painful reminder. Running the bases, he would slide hard into a bag and come up with blood oozing through his pants from his buttocks, where the cross had dug in deeply.

Skizas also had a habit of walking in his sleep, a practice that alarmed Bill Gabler, one of his minor league roommates. Gabler was careful to reposition his body before he went to sleep, turning 180 degrees so that his head was at the foot of the bed. Why? "So if Lou goes sleepwalking and tries to strangle me," Gabler said, "he'll strangle my feet."

Rico Carty

Pat Gillick was the general manager of the Toronto Blue Jays in 1978. For spring training, the team arranged for staff and players to stay at a Ramada Inn in Clearwater, Florida.

One morning Gillick was strolling through the hotel lobby when he was stopped by the facility's manager. "We think that your DH is trying to burn our hotel down," the gentleman stated tersely.

The befuddled Gillick demanded an explanation. Rico Carty, the Blue Jays' designated hitter, was new to the team and Gillick did not know him well.

Gillick soon discovered that Carty was practicing a fire ritual in his hotel room, and that the frightened maids had reported the practice to the manager.

Every day, Carty would fill the bathtub and the sink with water, and remove the top of the toilet water tank. He would then place two floating candles in the bathtub, two in the toilet tank and one in the sink, and light them before heading off to work.

The significance of five burning candles? For the superstitious Carty, each represented a base hit in the game that day. Of course, he didn't always get five hits, but "The Big Boy"—Carty's nickname for himself—batted better than .300 eight times in a 15-year major league career that ended in 1979.

Ramada Inn
Clearwater, Florida

Paul Konerko

The digital Rally Monkey jumps up and down on the Los Angeles Angels' JumboTron, invoking crowd support for the home team. The little fella first appeared in June 2000 and was an instant hit, so popular that it spawned a website and licensed souvenir items.

Paul Konerko's mother bought a stuffed version of the Rally Monkey early in the 2001 season and presented it to her son, the Chicago White Sox's first baseman, for good luck. But apparently the monkey works only for the Angels.

Konerko batted .152 in May. His father, in a fit of fury, grabbed Paul's Rally Monkey by the neck, beat it severely, burned it and unceremoniously dumped it in the trash. Almost on cue, Konerko emerged from his slump. He batted .356 for June and finished the season with 99 RBI.

"That's all my dad," Konerko said of the monkey assault. "He's like me. I go up there with a brand-new pair of batting gloves and make an out, and I throw 'em in the stands. I think anybody who's a golfer can relate. You make changes sometimes, and you feel better about it, you feel positive.

"Of course, it's not like it's the batting gloves' fault. But if you throw them away and get new ones, you think 'OK, I'm ready now.' Of course, it makes no sense. But baseball players do strange things like that." Often, assisted by those close to them.

CRUNCH

Raul Mondesi

Playing on the same team with outfielder Raul Mondesi can be hazardous to your health. It is surprising that some of his teammates have not suffered from dehydration for lack of having a cup to drink from in the dugout.

"He is the epitome of superstition," said Trenidad Hubbard, who played with Mondesi on the Los Angeles Dodgers in 1998 and 1999. "One of the things he has to do is step on every cup in the dugout to make sure it is smashed."

One can imagine Mondesi's exasperated teammates on a hot day, standing in a sea of crushed Styrofoam, drinking liquid from their cupped hands.

When he's the first batter in an inning, Mondesi—a member of the Atlanta Braves in 2005—is particularly pressed for time. In addition to his cup-stomping ritual, he has to tend to his equipment.

"When he's leading off an inning, he has to place his cap on top of his glove until it looks just right," Hubbard said. "He might do it 10 times before he can walk away. But that hat has to be just right before he'll go up to hit."

Hal Morris

Hal Morris was a slick-fielding first baseman for the Cincinnati Reds in the 1990s—a rookie on the 1990 team that swept the heavily favored Oakland Athletics in the World Series.

Before he signed a pro contract, Morris was using a Regent brand glove that he had purchased at a discount store. That glove never left his possession. He used it in the minor leagues and through-out his major league career. Even after the leather had worn thin and torn in several places, and the padding was gone in the pocket, Morris steadfastly refused to part with his treasured mitt.

One spring Morris' teammates convinced him to try a new glove, and he broke it in during spring training. On opening day, using the new glove, Morris made an error. The next day, the trusty Regent was back on his right hand, never again to be abandoned by Morris, who retired as a player in 2000.

Through 13 seasons, more than 8,100 chances as a first baseman, Morris made only 52 errors, never more than nine in a season.

13	SEASONS
8,127	CHANCES
52	ERRORS

David Cone

David Cone was one of the best and most confident pitchers of his era, a Cy Young Award winner and a five-time All-Star. But when the games got really important, he made certain to wear his lucky coat to the ballpark. It was a faded and stained brown bomber jacket, with a Labatt's beer crest on the breast.

Cone wore it to Atlanta's Fulton County Stadium on October 24, 1992, the night the Toronto Blue Jays won their first World Series by defeating the Braves 4-3 in 11 innings. Cone pitched six innings and gave up one run.

Four years later, Cone arrived at the same ballpark wearing the same grimy jacket, this time with the New York Yankees. It was the third game of the 1996 World Series, and the Yankees had lost the first two at home. Cone pitched his team to a 5-2 victory that night, the first of four straight wins for New York.

"I may not have the same locker this time," Cone said after his 1996 victory, "but I figured why not wear the thing? It has champagne stains on it from when we won the Series here with the Blue Jays. I may go out and have a Canadian beer right now to celebrate."

Don Robinson

Don Robinson was a reliable starting pitcher for four teams from 1978 to 1992, probably because he faithfully adhered to a few simple guidelines for success, such as:

1. Not allowing anyone to pick up the ball and hand it to him to start an inning. "Tim Raines was the worst," Robinson said, speaking of the outfielder who was his teammate in Montreal. "He would roll the ball somewhere near second base after our third out. I'd have to walk out there and pick it up."

2. Never touching the resin bag. "We didn't have resin bags when I was growing up in West Virginia," Robinson said. "The last time I touched one was in 1976 in the minors in Charleston. My next pitch, the batter hit a grand slam."

3. Always placing his cap and glove between innings on the dugout shelf just above the head of manager Roger Craig, when Robinson played for the San Francisco Giants. "I always had good luck with that spot," Robinson said.

51

Roy Halladay

Virtually every starting pitcher in the major leagues has a strict routine that he follows on the day he is scheduled to pitch. Some are such creatures of habit that even a slight variation in their game-day ritual can spin them into a near-convulsive state. Roy Halladay, who won the 2003 American League Cy Young Award pitching for the Toronto Blue Jays, is typical.

Halladay arrives at the ballpark precisely at 1 P.M. and schedules himself almost to the second, right up until he steps on the mound. At 6:15, for instance, he goes to the training room for a rubdown from the team trainer.

The session lasts 23½ minutes, and it must be done in complete silence.

When the trainer is finished, he washes his hands while Halladay waits. Then the pitcher pulls on his sweatshirt—he must have it on before he leaves the room. When Halladay is on his third step out the door, it is the trainer's responsibility to tell him, "Have a good one, Doc," referring to the pitcher by his nickname.

Rheal Cormier

When Tim Worrell joined the Philadelphia Phillies before the 2004 season, he and Rheal Cormier quickly became close friends. Since both were veteran relief pitchers, they shared a lot of time together.

It wasn't long before the highly superstitious Cormier had pulled Worrell into some of his routines. Cormier insisted that they walk to the bullpen together at the same time during every game. That afforded Worrell an opportunity to gently poke fun at his friend.

"Sometimes he pushes it," Cormier said. "He'll say, 'Let's wait another half-inning.' And I'm like, 'No, we have to go right now.'"

When he's not pitching well, Cormier will attempt to change his luck by throwing away all his baseball clothing and replacing it with new apparel. He did that on one occasion, only to have Worrell secretively retrieve the garments and return them to Cormier's locker. "The next day I was thinking, Didn't I throw that stuff away?" Cormier said.

The left-handed Cormier has many rituals. He starts each day with six pieces of gum and pops two into his mouth precisely at the start of the game. When he enters a game, he never uses the ball that's been left on the mound and always asks for a new one. Cormier doesn't like the catcher to touch the new ball, and often has to remind Phillies catcher Mike Lieberthal not to.

"I think it all depends on how good you're going," Cormier said of practicing his rituals. "If things are going well, I try to get to the park at the same time every day, do my running in the outfield exactly the same way, that sort of thing."

Relievers are entitled to eight warm-up pitches when they enter a game. Sometimes, though, an umpire tries to speed up the game by cutting them short. This bothers Cormier, who likes to throw exactly the same sequence of pitches each time he gets to the mound. "It throws me off a little bit when that doesn't happen," he said.

Cormier doesn't like anyone to handle his glove. "One time I picked up his glove and put it on," said Cormier's teammate Randy Wolf. "He was so bitter."

> **"One time I picked up his glove and put it on. He was so bitter."**

TRASH FOR
RHEAL
CORMIER'S
JINXED
UNIFORMS

Duane Ward

On his first day with the Toronto Blue Jays, September 1, 1986, relief pitcher Duane Ward put on a brand-new undershirt with blue sleeves, then pulled his uniform jersey over it. More than 1,000 games and as many washing-machine cycles later, Ward was still wearing that same Russell Athletic Wear.

By 1993, the garment was tattered almost beyond repair. "Every time he washes it," said fellow reliever Mark Eichhorn, "you can see the holes getting bigger and bigger."

An umpire told Ward that the holes were exposing his skin through the blue sleeves, creating a distraction to hitters. "I figure if a guy is looking at holes in my sleeves near my elbow, he's probably distracted anyway," Ward said. Nonetheless, he and the Toronto equipment man got out needle and thread and dutifully mended the holes, a chore that became increasingly frequent.

"You look at it, and it appears as if it's rotting away before your very eyes," said Blue Jays coach Bob Bailor.

Never changing his undershirt was just part of Ward's ritual. Leaving the bullpen to enter a game, Ward always spit out his gum on the warning track. He stutter-stepped across the white marking that defined the infield on artificial turf fields.

When the batboy approached to take his warm-up jacket, Ward tossed it to the lad, never handing it to him. And once he got to the mound, Ward always took the ball from his manager in his glove, never with his bare hand.

Ward didn't dare mess with his routine. As a setup man for closer Tom Henke from 1988 to 1992, Ward was one of the most dependable relievers in the major leagues, averaging 73 appearances and 113 innings for those five seasons. In 1993 he replaced Henke and led the American League in saves with 45.

Big Ed Walsh

In the days of the legal spitball, Big Ed Walsh, a Hall of Fame pitcher for the Chicago White Sox, habitually rubbed the ball against his tongue and lower lip. He then licked it and delivered a pitch.

Noticing Walsh's habit and aware of his propensity for winning—40 victories in 1908, 27 in both 1911 and 1912—Philadelphia Athletics manager Connie Mack ingeniously prepared for the pitcher's start against his team one day. Mack procured a bucketful of horse manure and rubbed some on the baseballs to be used in the game. Walsh began licking the ball as soon as he took the mound. He vomited throughout the game and was ineffective, and the A's won easily.

Three days later, Walsh pitched against the A's again, and Mack pulled the same trick.

Word of the dung-smeared baseballs quickly spread to other teams, who adopted the practice. Soon Walsh was unable to put his lips to any ball without impulsively vomiting. While he could have employed other means to moisten the ball for a spitter, Walsh chose none. He was just 31 at the outset of the 1913 season, yet struggled for the rest of his career, pitching in only 34 games and winning only 13 from 1913 to 1917.

Some said his arm was dead from overuse—he pitched an extraordinary 886 innings during the 1907 and 1908 seasons. Others believed he could have continued to be effective if not for his aversion to licking baseballs, brought on by Mack's shenanigans.

GRADE D HORSE MANURE

Brian Holton

Brian Holton, a relief pitcher for the Los Angeles Dodgers and Baltimore Orioles from 1985 to 1990, had to do everything in the same sequence when he was pitching.

"He wouldn't take the ball out of your hand," said Rick Dempsey, a catcher with the Orioles when Holton was with the team. "He wiped the rubber four times with his right foot, four times with his left foot, took eight warm-up pitches, then did a 360-degree turn and entered the mound from the back.

"In the dugout, he had to sit at the left of the catcher, and he always took two swigs of water before taking the mound."

Was Dempsey telling the truth?

"He left out the good parts," Holton said. "I got dressed the same way every day. Then I would button just three buttons of my warm-up jacket. I'd get a towel and wrap it around my neck, and the tag always had to be on the right side.

"I put two cans of Copenhagen in my pocket, one from spring training and a new one.

"In my left pocket, I carried a lasso. I found a piece of rope in San Diego in 1988 and made a lasso out of it, and we went on a winning streak, so I always kept it with me on the field after that.

"I'd sit in the same seat in the bullpen and in the dugout. I'd come up on the mound from the first base side. I'd wipe the pitching rubber four times with each leg and spin around clockwise. I'd catch the ball with one foot on the dirt and one foot on the grass.

"I'd never warm up between innings with anybody except my catcher. If he'd been the last batter and was getting on his gear, I'd wait for him. I wouldn't throw to anyone else."

Any other quirky behavior?

"Oh yeah, I'd always sing to myself on the mound to whatever music was being played over the PA system," Holton said. "If they weren't playing anything, I'd sing, 'You take the high road, I'll take the low road.'"

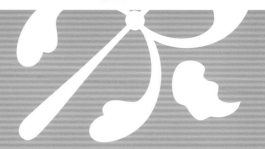

Ron Santo

Ron Santo, the Chicago Cubs great third baseman of the 1960s and 1970s, sat down one morning during the 1966 season and, as usual, had eggs for breakfast. This time, he also ate canned fruit cocktail. "I'd never done that before," he said.

In the coming weeks, Santo eagerly gulped down fruit cocktail each morning. He was hitting particularly well at the time, mounting a hitting streak that would reach 28 games, the best of his career. What did hitting well have to do with fruit cocktail for breakfast? Santo didn't know, but he certainly wasn't interested in finding out.

When the hitting streak ended, fruit cocktail also disappeared from Santo's breakfast fare.

Dave Concepcion

On the bus trip from their downtown Chicago hotel to Wrigley Field, visiting baseball teams pass the intersection at Belmont Avenue and Sheridan Road. There sits a statue of Civil War–era Gen. Philip H. Sheridan and his horse Winchester rearing into the air. This is the same General Sheridan who gained notoriety for saying, "The only good Indian is a dead Indian" and, "If I owned Texas and Hell, I would rent out Texas and live in Hell."

During the 1970s and 1980s, a visiting team's rookie players were dispatched to General Sheridan's statue late at night to paint the horse's testicles the team's colors for good luck. If you happened to be passing by, you knew which team was in town to play the Cubs by the color of Winchester's testicles.

One day in the 1970s, the Cincinnati Reds were approaching Belmont and Sheridan when shortstop Dave Concepcion, a highly superstitious man, implored the bus driver to stop. Concepcion was in the throes of a horrible batting slump and willing to try almost anything to change his fortunes. He hopped off the bus, climbed the statue and—much to the amusement of teammates and to the amazement of gawking pedestrians—planted a firm kiss on the horse's testicles.

Alas, Concepcion went 0-for-5 that day. He tried another tack after the game, taking a shower while wearing his Reds uniform—"To wash away the slump," he explained. As a gag, Concepcion then climbed into an industrial-sized clothes dryer and closed the door. Pitcher Pat Zachry, without a word, approached the dryer and hit the ON switch.

Those Reds have a lasting memory of Concepcion spinning around and around behind the large glass door, a terrified expression on his face. When someone let him out, every hair on his body was singed.

The Chicago police eventually put an end to the testicle-painting ritual, although the Reds and others continue to be known as ballplayers.

Rob Murphy

Rob Murphy was a highly effective—if slightly eccentric—left-handed relief pitcher for eight teams in his 11-year major league career. He pitched for the Cincinnati Reds from 1985 to 1988, often wearing a pair of women's black silk panties under his athletic supporter. Asked for an explanation, Murphy grinned slyly and said, "I've worn them ever since my girlfriend found them in the glove compartment, and they weren't hers."

Actually, Murphy said, a friend gave him the panties, and he wore them under his uniform one day as a gag. He pitched well that day, so he continued to wear the frilly undergarment. Every time it crossed his mind that he was doing something ridiculous, Murphy would pitch in such outstanding fashion that he knew instinctively he always would be pitching in women's panties.

"I look at it as my security blanket," Murphy said. "You can't see them; nobody but me knows they're on. But they're important. I have certain things I do to get ready for the game—go over hitters, warm up, etc.—and putting on the underwear is part of that, part of my mental preparation."

What if he started pitching badly on a consistent basis? "Are you kidding me?" Murphy asked. "I'd take them off in a second and throw them away."

Brad Ausmus

Houston Astros catcher Brad Ausmus steadfastly claims that he has no superstitions, nothing to the point where "if I don't do something, it changes the whole karma of my life."

On second thought, Ausmus acknowledges that he does have one ritual that he practices religiously. It comes from years and years of coaches and instructors drilling into him that a successful catcher has to be able to separate his offense from his defense.

"For as long as I can remember," Ausmus says, "when I get to the circle of dirt where home plate is, as I'm crossing over from the grass to the dirt, I put my mask on. That's like my mental trigger to forget about the offense and now move to the defense. When I'm stepping onto the dirt, I do it."

Steve McCatty

Steve McCatty pitched from 1977 to 1985 for the Oakland Athletics and left Major League Baseball with a 63-63 record. He was a 14-game winner twice and a 14-game loser twice. No matter whether he was going good or going bad, one thing remained constant: He never stepped on a baseline. It was a ritual born in his high school days and followed religiously until his final game.

"I'd always hop over the line," McCatty said. "Left leg first. I'd never use the right leg. I'd do it that way going out and coming in."

Once back in the dugout, McCatty also followed a ritual with his equipment. He would take off his cap, pull on his jacket and place his glove on his left knee. "With two outs, I'd take my jacket off," he said.

Back on the mound, McCatty would make his allotted eight warm-up tosses to the catcher, wait for the ball to be returned to him after being thrown around the infield, then instinctively flip it to the umpire in exchange for a new ball.

McCatty was wary of striking out too many batters. "If I struck out the side, I always had a bad next inning," he said.

"So I tried not to do that." He had 541 strikeouts for his major league career, averaging just 4.1 per nine innings. No telling how many he might have had if he had been trying.

"You're always trying to find that little something that helps you," McCatty said. "It sounds stupid, but I'd keep doing that if I was still playing. I'd keep riding it out."

Larry Walker

Larry Walker's favorite number is three. He has worn number 33 on his uniform as a member of the Montreal Expos, Colorado Rockies and St. Louis Cardinals. He puts the weight doughnut on his bat in the on-deck circle and takes three swings, or six or nine—always multiples of three. He sets his alarm clock for three minutes past the hour. He takes a shower under the third nozzle in the clubhouse facility.

Walker said he began engaging in ritualistic activity in 1987 while in the minor leagues. He was searching for a routine, something that allowed him pause and comfort, no matter the surroundings or the time zone.

"I used to always tie one of my shoes when I was in the on-deck circle whether I needed to or not," Walker said. "I'd untie one of my shoes and tie it back up. It got to the point that sometimes it was a struggle to untie a shoe and tie it back up, because I had too much pine tar on my hand, or else a shoelace would get caught in my batting glove. And I'd do a double knot.

"So I abandoned that and went to carving my girlfriend's initials in the on-deck circle. I'd carve her initials and circle them. She dumped me, so I got rid of that one. My favorite number is three so I tried three practice swings. Ever since, it's been three of everything, multiples of three usually."

Walker's obsession with the number three isn't likely to change, not with a career batting average that begins with that numeral. His .314 mark entering the 2005 season ranked seventh among active major league players.

Walker said he will do something like tap his foot with his bat, realize he has done it twice and do it again, "whether I like it or not." Much of what he does in threes is not "a lot of laid out bookwork stuff that I have to follow, but more impromptu: I'm at two; well, I've got to do one more."

Up to a point, that is. Walker is married to his second wife and said that he doesn't plan to have a third. In matters of the heart, number three has not always boded well for Walker.

"I got married in '93, on November 3, at 3:33 P.M.," he said. "We were married for three years. I got divorced, and she got $3 million."

015

013

DATE _____

Larry Walker's Ex-Wife $ 3,000,000.00

Three Million Dollars and 00/100   100 DOLLARS 🔒 Security features included. Details on back.

40576

Larry Walker

MP

_____

Bazooka

BUBBLE GUM

Dwight Gooden

Chomp, chomp, chomp. Check and see how things are going. Chomp, chomp, chomp. Gauge things again.

Oh, sorry—that was just Dwight Gooden testing his luck back in his heyday in the 1980s and early 1990s. Like many other players, Gooden was superstitious enough that he refused to step on the chalk lines as he trotted on and off the field. But there was something else with Gooden, something a little more subtle: If he lost a game, or if his luck turned sour during a game, he changed the chewing gum.

Good old-fashioned Bazooka was his base. "But if that wouldn't work, I'd switch to other gum, like Juicy Fruit," Gooden said. "I did that my whole career."

The chewing gum ritual started when Gooden was in the minor leagues. "I don't know what brought it on," he said. "I was giving up a lot of runs one day, so I just spit it out and tried another flavor. It worked, so I kept doing it. I'd switch over to Juicy Fruit, Bubblicious, something like that."

Gooden also wanted a certain bullpen catcher to warm him up. Mike Borzello, who remains a bullpen catcher in New York to this day, served Gooden well during the latter part of his career with the Yankees.

Joe Torre

Sometimes it's wise to hold back on a superstition until you really need it. And because New York Yankees manager Joe Torre did just that, the San Diego Padres never knew that an Italian restaurant in Westchester County, New York, conspired against them in the 1998 World Series.

Torre, as a player, never bothered much with any of that superstition stuff. During an 18-year career with the Milwaukee and Atlanta Braves, St. Louis Cardinals and New York Mets, he was selected for the All-Star Game nine times without the benefit of any juju or witchcraft.

"But as a manager, sometimes you have such a helpless feeling," he said. Consequently, Torre sticks with the same jersey or warm-up top if the Yankees are winning. If you notice him in the dugout wearing a navy blue windbreaker with the NY logo on the front for multiple games, chances are the Yanks have won two or three in a row, and Torre isn't about to test his luck. Same with a jersey—he wears the one he had on at the onset of a winning streak.

Except for choosing his uniform garments according to the Yankees' fortunes, Torre doesn't indulge in superstitious behavior. Oh, there was that occasion during the 1998 World Series when Torre requested help from an Italian friend before ever motioning for ace closer Mariano Rivera from the bullpen.

Earlier in the postseason, Torre had eaten a game-day lunch at a family-style Italian restaurant called La Riserva, near his home in Larchmont. The Yankees won that night, so before Game 1 of the World Series with the Padres, Torre planned to go to La Riserva again.

But La Riserva was not open for lunch on Saturday. No problem. The restaurant owners told Torre, "You come for lunch." Torre did, and later that night the Yankees served up a 9-6 victory and went on to sweep the Padres for their second World Series championship under Torre.

Ken Griffey Jr.

When Ken Griffey Jr.'s bat slows down and the hits stop falling, it isn't good news for Cincinnati Reds fans—but it is good news for area freight services.

If Griffey doesn't get a hit when the Reds are playing at home, he often will drive a different car from his fleet to the ballpark the following day. And on at least one occasion, a deep slump inspired Griffey to reduce the size of his fleet.

"I shipped a car to my home in Florida because I didn't get a hit with it for a month," Griffey said, recalling a Mercedes that he banished from Cincinnati. "Every time I drove it, I didn't get a hit. My best friend looked at me like, 'What?'"

Griffey became so disgusted with the car that he later traded it in for another Mercedes. Presumably, that one came stocked with hits—Griffey still has it.

As a practitioner of quirky behavior, Griffey ranks himself between "Extremely Superstitious" and "Really Superstitious." For one thing, when his turn to bat comes, he walks to the plate the same way every time.

"If we're on the first-base side, I take a straight line to the box, and I don't touch the foul line," said Griffey of his route to the left-handed batter's box. "If we're on the third-base side, I'll walk around the umpire, like a horseshoe, and try to walk into the same spot as if I was on the first-base side."

Griffey also clings firmly to another ritual. When fans throw money onto the field, he never leaves it. Griffey long ago started picking up coins and depositing them into his fielder's glove. The lacing on the wrist strap makes a good coin holder.

"When I played on Astroturf in Seattle, you'd see coins bouncing and then rolling," Griffey said. "You'd grab it and stick it in your glove. Jay Buhner did the same thing. When our gloves got filled, we'd try to find another outfielder to do it." How much money has this practice netted Griffey over the years? "I've made a few dollars," he said, laughing.

Though Griffey's salaries over the years made him a multimillionaire, the extra cash can come in handy when, say, he feels the need to dispose of a light-hitting luxury automobile.

Pedro Borbon

Pedro Borbon was a relief pitcher for the Cincinnati
Reds throughout the 1970s, an integral part of their
World Championship teams of 1975 and 1976. Once the
baseball season was over, he returned to his native
country, the Dominican Republic, where he supplemented
his income by raising fighting cocks.

Borbon was known for his strong and sharp teeth. If the rawhide strips used to string together the fingers of a baseball glove were too long, a clubhouse attendant would bring the glove to Borbon and he would gladly bite off the excess leather.

The Reds and the New York Mets once engaged in a melee. As order was being restored, Borbon picked up a cap and put it on his head—but it belonged to the Mets' Cleon Jones. When he realized his mistake, Borbon angrily yanked the cap off his head, and bit a hunk out of the bill and chewed it up.

Borbon practiced voodoo. When the Reds released him in 1979, he placed a curse on the team and proclaimed, "They'll never win another World Series."

The curse held through the 1980s. When the Reds won the National League pennant in 1990, several members of the Cincinnati media contacted Borbon, wondering whether he would consider lifting the curse. He did, and the Reds swept the heavily favored Oakland Athletics in the World Series.

Shortly after, Borbon reinstated his curse, and the Reds haven't been back to the World Series since.

Albert Belle

Albert Belle was one of the most feared men in the major leagues in the 1990s, a scourge to pitchers and a menace to sportswriters. He also was the son that could make any mother proud.

Belle was a neat freak.

The man would not think of playing in a baseball game until everything was in perfect order in his locker. His shoes had to be shined and in perfect alignment at the foot of his locker. His T-shirts, first the white ones, then the grays, hung neatly next to his uniform jerseys. His fielder's gloves were arranged on the top shelf as if they were on display in a sporting goods store. His chair had to face the door of the clubhouse.

"Everything had to be perfect with him," said Omar Vizquel, who played with Belle on the Cleveland Indians for three seasons. "Everything from his locker to how he played soft-toss. It was ridiculous.

"But you know what? It worked."

If it worked for Belle—he slugged 381 home runs and batted .295 in his 12-year career that ended in 2000—why not try it

yourself?

"I started copying him when I played with him In Chicago," said San Francisco Giants reliever Scott Eyre, referring to the White Sox and the 1997 and 1998 seasons. "I started pointing my chair toward the clubhouse door. It has to be that way every day. If somebody sits in it and moves it, I get pissed. I line my shoes up in my locker, too, like Albert did.

"When I started my superstitions to be like Albert, I asked him, 'What difference does it make how your shoes are lined up in a locker?'

"He told me, 'Kid, if you're ever going to have success in this game, you have to have some routine in your life.'

"Made sense to me. Something's working. I'm still in the big leagues."

Kevin Millar

Boston Red Sox first baseman and outfielder Kevin Millar has probably never encountered a superstition or ritual that he didn't think was worth a try. Anything to hit a baseball harder and more frequently, or to promote team camaraderie and harmony.

Millar once sported long hair and chin stubble in tribute to the 1993 Philadelphia Phillies, a rollicking, throwback team that won the National League pennant. For the 2003 playoffs, Millar shaved his head close in keeping with the spirit of the "Cowboy Up" movement he fostered among the Red Sox.

Millar will keep his stirrup socks pulled high for weeks on end if he thinks it's helping him at the plate, or do the opposite if he thinks that look will engender good fortune.

But for sheer weirdness, nothing comes close to a ritual that Millar practiced during spring training with the Florida Marlins in 2000. It seems that one of his Beaumont, Texas, hunting buddies had an idea to make Millar a better hitter. (Millar attended Lamar University in Beaumont and likes the town so much that he lives there in the offseason.)

The buddy gave Millar a couple of vials of doe urine—how it was acquired is probably a good story, too—with instructions to sprinkle it on his bats. The urine, the buddy claimed, would make the bats less likely to shatter. Who knows? Maybe doe urine would attract horsehide as well. Millar blessed his bats regularly with the liquid waste that spring, and he hit so well that he won a place in the Marlins' Opening Day lineup as the first baseman.

Good teammate that he is, Millar shared the urine with Mike Redmond and Mike Lowell for their bats, too. By mid-April, not only Millar was out of doe urine, but the whole Marlins lineup. He played sparingly the rest of the season and batted .259, his lowest average in the major leagues.

John Kruk

As a player, John Kruk was as well known for his ample girth as for his quick wit and .300 batting average.

Kruk, now a baseball analyst for ESPN, indulged in several superstitions. When he was hitting well, he would not change his uniform socks. When he went into a slump, he would change them daily.

Kruk played for the Philadelphia Phillies from 1989 to 1994. He apparently disliked the team's ballpark or hated going to work, or both. When he drove to Veterans Stadium, he would scream obscenities as the ballpark came into view.

Former teammates remember Kruk fondly for his dining fare. If the man looked like he trained on Budweiser and mashed potatoes, it was because that wasn't far from the truth. Kruk frequently sent clubhouse attendants on pregame food runs to fast food restaurants. What he ordered depended on how the Phillies had fared in the previous game.

A five-game winning streak meant that Kruk had the same fare from the same joint for five straight pregame meals. When the team lost, he would change restaurants. Burger King, McDonald's, Kentucky Fried Chicken, Pizza Hut and a local cheesesteak joint were in the regular rotation.

Needless to say, a steady diet of burgers and fries tends to pack on the pounds. But the portly Kruk never seemed too concerned. Once, when he looked heavier than usual, a reporter asked Kruk if he was in shape.

"To run a marathon? Probably not," he conceded. "To play baseball? Yeah, I'll be all right."

RADIO

"I didn't play enoug to be superstitio

TRANSISTOR

ON ▶

Rusty Staub

When Lynn Jones was a rookie with the Detroit Tigers in 1979, Rusty Staub was in the 17th season of a major league career that ended in 1985. It didn't take Jones long to notice that Staub took a nap at the same time daily, always sleeping in a small room off the media dining room at Tiger Stadium.

Napping on schedule wasn't the only part of Staub's baseball ritual. He kept his bats in a separate bag, so they would never touch those of his teammates. Staub, the Tigers' designated hitter in 1979 until being traded to the Montreal Expos in July, also followed a precise pattern after each of his at-bats.

"Between at-bats, his shoes had to be brushed off, and there had to be no dirt on the cleats," Jones said. "When he finished his at-bat, he would go to the clubhouse, listen to the game on TV or radio and do his crossword puzzle."

When Staub's spikes were cleaned, Jones said, "they had to be placed in the same spot beside his locker." One inning before his next at-bat, Staub would return to the bench and study the pitcher. "He would know every little idiosyncrasy—hand position, every little movement," Jones said.

The young Jones studied all the veterans, trying to find out what works in the big leagues. He could have patterned himself after Staub, who had 2,716 hits in 23 major league seasons, except for one problem: "I didn't play enough to be superstitious."

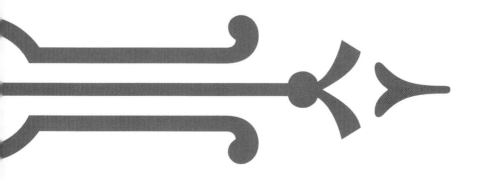

Roberto Hernandez

Mick Billmeyer didn't know what hit him, and hit him again, over and over.

Billmeyer, the Philadelphia Phillies catching instructor, was warming up Roberto Hernandez for the first time since the veteran relief pitcher joined the team in 2004. Billmeyer was having a tough time of it, with more balls glancing off his body than he caught.

Every pitch that Hernandez threw seemed to break in a different direction. Some dove, some sailed. Billmeyer, who had been a catcher in the minor leagues for eight years, had never seen anything quite like this before. It was only later that he found out what was going on.

It seems that Hernandez doesn't like to warm up in the bullpen with just any baseballs. He has his favorites. Once he finds one he likes, he puts it in a ball bag and uses it over and over again.

Frequently used baseballs pick up assorted scuffs and nicks. And as every pitcher who has ever doctored a baseball knows, even the slightest blemish can cause a ball's flight to be wildly unpredictable.

Finding out that it wasn't entirely his fault that he was having so much trouble catching Hernandez's pitches helped soothe Billmeyer's bruised ego. But it didn't do much for the bruises on his arms and legs.

Randy Wolf

Philadelphia Phillies left-hander Randy Wolf is a laid-back Southern Californian. Nothing seems to bother him. Well, almost nothing.

When Wolf is the starting pitcher and is seated in the dugout while the Phillies are batting, he keeps a towel nearby that he doesn't want anyone to touch. Yet, invariably he'll catch shortstop Jimmy Rollins reaching for it.

"Don't touch that," Wolf will bark.

"Aw, I forgot," Rollins will reply with a grin.

Without fail, Wolf brings two towels from the clubhouse to the dugout on the days that he pitches. One is to wrap around his left arm between innings, the other is to wipe his face. When he's done with the face towel, he places it carefully on the bench, and no one else is allowed to use it.

Wolf doesn't think Rollins reaches for his towel intentionally, but that the shortstop simply forgets, although they have been teammates since 2000.

Anyway, why would an apparently sensible person care about a teammate touching his towel?

"You know what it is?" Wolf said. "How many times have you seen a pitcher throw the ball right down the middle, and it gets popped up? There are so many things in this game that you can't control. That's where superstitions come in—trying to control things that are out of your control."

John Smoltz

John Smoltz has been a 24-game winner as a starting pitcher and a 55-saves closer during his remarkable career with the Atlanta Braves that entered its 17th season in 2005 ... and to think that he might not always have been in tiptop shape when he took the pitcher's mound. Listen to Mark Grant, Smoltz's teammate for part of the 1990 season:

"Smoltzie had started doing jumping jacks right before the Braves scored the first run. They ended up having a big inning that went on for nearly 20 minutes, and he never stopped. He kept telling Tom Glavine, 'I can't stop! I can't stop!'"

On another occasion, Smoltz must have had a Babe Ruth–sized bellyache when he left the dugout for the mound.

"He was eating chicken wings, and the Braves had a big inning," Grant said. "He ended up eating, like, 40 wings."

Billy Williams

Billy Williams had 2,711 hits during a stellar 18-year career with the Chicago Cubs and Oakland Athletics that gained him entry into the baseball Hall of Fame. As well as he hit a baseball, Williams was even more adept at swatting a wad of chewing gum.

Before stepping into the batter's box, Williams always made a point of spitting out the half stick of gum in his mouth and taking a swing at it. Almost without exception, his bat would meet the gum. Only then was he ready to hit.

"I would walk around home plate, and I'd spit the gum up and hit it into the opposing team's dugout," Williams said. "You'd see guys ducking. I always did it. Every at-bat I did it. I figured if I could hit that little piece of gum, I should be able to hit the baseball."

Years later Joe Carter, who began his career in the Cubs organization, adopted a similar ritual. But no one did it as well as Williams. On those rare occasions when he fanned at his gum, he wouldn't pick it up; he would keep right on going. "I don't remember those times," he said. "I don't remember missing it that many times. I had it down pat when I hit that gum. When I spit it out, I'd just whale it."

Williams didn't consider himself particularly superstitious when he played, although he always made sure to step over the baseline with his right foot first. That practice, however, paled in comparison with his spit-and-hit ritual.

"It started out a habit," he said. "Then when you do things for so long, it becomes a superstition. If you don't do it, you feel you're not carrying out everything that you should do to hit a baseball."

PHILLIES WIN
THE WORLD
SERIES!

Mike Schmidt
and Tug McGraw

Third baseman Mike Schmidt and relief pitcher Tug
McGraw were Philadelphia Phillies teammates during
the 1980 season and lived near each other in a subur-
ban area. They rode together to Veterans Stadium for
home games.

A routine quickly developed. Schmidt would drive, and on the way to the park they would stop at the same convenience store, where McGraw would buy a Frank's lime soda. As the season wore on and the Phillies moved closer to winning the National League East championship, Schmidt and McGraw drove ever so carefully and never passed their favorite convenience store without stopping.

The Phillies not only won the division championship, but also the National League pennant, and met the Kansas City Royals in the World Series. Before Game 6, Schmidt and McGraw fantasized about what would happen if the Phillies won that night and clinched the first World Series championship for the 98-year-old franchise.

The more they talked, the more a plan began to take shape. McGraw felt certain that he would be on the mound in the ninth inning. Schmidt mentioned that photographers focused on the celebration near the mound after the final out. Schmidt asked McGraw to wait for him after the final out was recorded, assuming McGraw would be on the mound.

Sure enough, McGraw was pitching in the top of the ninth. McGraw struck out Willie Wilson with the bases loaded to clinch the Phillies' 4-1 victory, leaped in jubilation and turned toward third base and braced for the arrival of Schmidt, who jumped into McGraw's arms.

A photo of Schmidt and McGraw's celebratory embrace made the cover of *Sports Illustrated* and remains an iconic image in Philadelphia history.

Terry Francona and Theo Epstein

When Terry Francona was the Philadelphia Phillies manager from 1997 to 2000, before a game he often emptied a packet of Metamucil into a half-full bottle of water, shook it, and chugged the concoction. He said the fiber laxative helped settle his stomach.

Francona resumed his Metamucil habit after becoming manager of the Boston Red Sox in 2004. In both Philadelphia and Boston, managing the local major league baseball team can make anyone's insides churn.

Red Sox general manager Theo Epstein was feeling a little queasy himself after the team fell behind the New York Yankees, three games to none, in the 2004 American League Championship Series. Before Game 4, with literally nothing left to lose, Epstein sat in the manager's office at Fenway Park and asked Francona to mix him a drink. Francona prepared two Metamucil cocktails, and the men drank them down.

The Red Sox won that night. The manager and the general manager shared their favorite drink before the next game, and the Red Sox won again. This went on

for eight straight games as Boston eliminated the Yankees in the greatest comeback in baseball history and swept the St. Louis Cardinals in the World Series.

"We went undefeated, but I paid the price," Epstein said. "It usually hit me around the eighth inning when the other team had runners in scoring position."

Epstein has an Ivy League education and a law degree. He places great stock in statistical analysis when making baseball decisions. But if it's a laxative shake that brings wins, he'll suck down as many as it takes. "It sounded like something for a 70-year-old grandmother, but I thought it might change our luck," Epstein said.

Francona not only became the first Red Sox manager to win a World Series in 86 years, but he also signed an endorsement deal with Metamucil.

Baseball Scouts

The Toronto Blue Jays dispatched a team of five scouts to the 1992 National League Championship Series to prepare reports on the Atlanta Braves and Pittsburgh Pirates. The reports would be invaluable to the Blue Jays should they win the American League pennant and go to the World Series.

On the morning of October 14, Blue Jays scouts Al LaMacchia, Moose Johnson, Chris Bourjos, Tim Wilken and Joe Ford gathered in a concierge lounge at the Atlanta Marriott Marquis. They had to attend the seventh game of the NL series that night, but first they would watch the Blue Jays on TV. Toronto was playing that afternoon, needing a victory to clinch their first pennant. Where should the scouts tune in?

"In 1991 when we were eliminated by Minnesota, we all watched in the same room in Atlanta," Johnson said. Obviously that hadn't done the Blue Jays any good.

"We tried a different strategy," Johnson said. "We each watched from our own room. Except LaMacchia. He was so

nervous he couldn't watch at all."

Wilken may have been alone in his room, but he reacted like a frenzied fan in the stands, screaming with joy when the Blue Jays' Candy Maldonado hit a home run, and Juan Guzman struck out Rickey Henderson with two runners on base.

The guest rooms at the 47-story Atlanta Marriott Marquis surround a soaring atrium. "I'm surprised security wasn't called to report there was a lunatic on the 46th floor, opening his door and screaming, 'We're going to the World Series!'" said Wilken, who was that lunatic.

Following the Blue Jays' 9-2 pennant-clinching victory, the scouts met in the lobby for high fives, hugs and tears.

"We might not have watched our game together," Wilken said, "but we were the last ones to leave the hospitality tent after the Braves won that night."

Wilken had expected the Blue Jays to reach the World Series since being awakened by a 1:30 A.M. telephone call in late August. The caller had told him the team was about to trade for pitcher David Cone, a significant acquisition.

"Anything wrong?" asked Wilken's wife after he hung up the phone. "Nope," he replied. "Just some guy phoning to say we're going to the World Series."

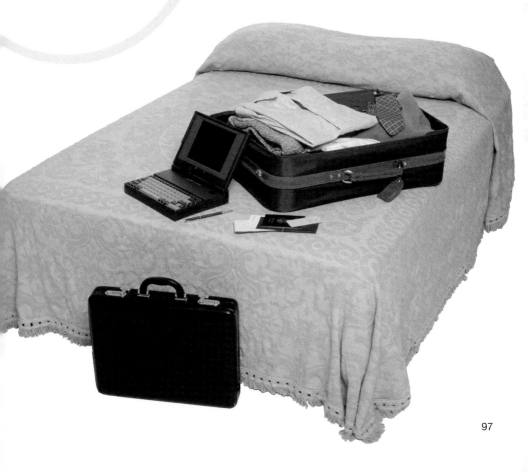

Nomar Garciaparra

Chicago Cubs shortstop Nomar Garciaparra refuses to acknowledge that he might be superstitious. He claims that he does not believe in curses, jinxes or hexes.

"I don't do the things I do because I'm superstitious," he said. "I do them out of habit. They're part of my routine. I've been doing them since I was in Little League."

Garciaparra engages in perhaps the most detailed and elaborate routine in the major leagues when he is at-bat. After every pitch, he steps out of the batter's box, adjusts his batting gloves and gives each a tug and touches his nose. When he steps back into the box, he carefully digs each foot into the dirt one at a time, taps his toes and shifts his weight back and forth from one foot to another.

"I like things tight when anything is on my feet or hands," Garciaparra said. "I do my toe tapping so my feet are at the ends of my shoes. Same thing with my hands— my gloves mustn't be loose at all. Before I exert any energy, my shoes and gloves have to be tight."

When he leaves the dugout for the playing field, Garciaparra makes certain to walk on each step with both feet. On the field, he frequently removes his fielder's glove from his left hand, smells the inside of the glove and his hand, and puts the glove back on.

When dressing for a game, Garciaparra is careful to put on each item of clothing in the same order that he has followed for as far back as he can remember. At precisely 15 minutes before the first pitch, he ritualistically signs autographs for fans near the dugout.

"I don't know why I do any of that stuff," Garciaparra said. "I just do it. It's not like I make myself do it."

A psychologist might determine that Garciaparra has an obsessive-compulsive disorder. If that's what it takes to be a .322 career hitter and a five-time All-Star in nine major league seasons—Garciaparra's achievement entering the 2005 season— then every ballplayer would likely attempt to contract the same disorder.

Jerry Royster

In 1975, Jerry Royster played for the Albuquerque Dukes, the Triple-A affiliate of the Los Angeles Dodgers. After every home game, he would leave his bats with three sisters, little girls named Deana, Laurie and Cheryl. They would take the bats home, clean them and bring them back the following day with a four-leaf clover.

Royster won the Pacific Coast League batting championship that season with a .333 average.

Royster went on to the major leagues—he played for five different teams over 16 seasons—but he kept in touch with the girls. It became a tradition that Royster would call them every year on Opening Day, and they would wish him good fortune for the coming season. "I never started a season without talking to them," he said.

One year Royster's team, the San Diego Padres, was in San Francisco on Opening Day when he realized he hadn't made his annual call. Two of the girls were in college, and he didn't know where to contact them. Deana, the youngest, was a senior in high school. He telephoned the high school. "Hi, this is Jerry Royster. I'm a baseball player for San Diego. I need to talk to Deana Kline. It's important."

"It caused a stir," Royster said.

The girl's mother had alerted the school that Royster might be calling. Deana was summoned to the school office, and she granted the ballplayer the annual good-luck wish that he had come to relish.

"One of the girls came with her parents and visited me in San Diego," Royster said. "We hadn't won in a while. But I got a pinch-hit to win the game. Sure, it maybe was a coincidence, but . . .

"They stayed at our house, didn't come to the next two or three games and we lost. The next time we brought them to a game, I hit a home run off a right-hander, and I hardly ever played against right-handers."

The girls continued to send Royster four-leaf clovers until he retired in 1988.

Shane Reynolds

Shane Reynolds, a major league pitcher from 1992 to 2004, was superstitious to the point that walking a straight line was virtually impossible for him.

Houston Astros catcher Brad Ausmus, a teammate of Reynolds' for four seasons, remembers that Reynolds took a certain number of steps around the pitcher's mound before starting an inning, then picked up the ball and touched his knuckles to the dirt. Reynolds then walked up on the mound and used his right foot to clean off the pitcher's rubber.

In the clubhouse at the Astrodome, Reynolds would not walk directly to the weight training room. Instead, he would walk around a laundry basket and then head to the weight room

"Finally I said to him, 'Shane, that is going to wear you out, having to remember all that stuff,'" Ausmus said. "And he goes, 'I hate the season. It drives me nuts.'"

Ausmus said he once pushed the laundry basket close to a locker, leaving little room between the basket and a chair. Undeterred, Reynolds walked toward the basket and wedged his way between it and the chair on his way to the weight room.

Reynolds' eccentricities were not limited to the playing field and the clubhouse. He once shared a hotel room on road trips with relief pitcher Todd Jones, and Jones soon discovered that his roommate maintained a strict fast-food ritual on the days he was scheduled to be the starting pitcher.

"Shane would have to go to Burger King on the day he pitched and get a Double Whopper with cheese, fries and a large Dr Pepper," Jones said. "Unless it was a day game. If it was a day game, he had to get the food the night before and put it in the refrigerator overnight."

Unfortunately, some hotel rooms do not have refrigerators, in which case Reynolds would leave the food on a table overnight and eat it the next morning before pitching that afternoon.

Jones sometimes awoke to the odor of day-old burgers and fries, but he didn't mind. "I knew Shane was going to have a good outing after that."

Reynolds was quite successful in his 11 seasons with the Astros. He had a 103-86 record, including 19 victories in 1998.

Julio Gotay

Julio Gotay kicked around the major leagues for 10 years as a utility infielder, playing shortstop and second base for four teams from 1960 to 1969. He had no remarkable skills, he was a career .260 hitter with six home runs and 70 RBI, yet his contemporaries light up in amusement when remembering him.

Gotay, a native of Puerto Rico, had a deep fear of crosses, whether it was two sticks placed across each other or two lines intersecting in the dirt. His phobia was widely known, and opponents tried to use it to their advantage.

In the late 1960s, Gotay and Elrod Hendricks, then a Baltimore Orioles catcher, played on the same winter ball team in Puerto Rico. Hendricks recalls a game when Gotay's superstition was particularly vexing. As a runner broke from first base, Hendricks pegged a quick throw to second base. Gotay, the shortstop, was supposed to cover the bag, but instead he remained frozen at his position, not twitching a muscle, and the ball bounded into center field. Shortly afterward, the same thing happened again—Hendricks threw to second, but Gotay didn't budge.

Hendricks stormed into the infield and soon found out what had happened. The other team had made a cross of chicken bones near second base, spooking Gotay and effectively rendering him useless for any plays in the vicinity.

Hendricks angrily stomped on the bones and kicked them away, much to the dismay of Gotay. With horror in his eyes, Gotay warned that bad luck was imminent.

"Sure enough, about three pitches later, Willie Montanez hit me in the back of the head on his backswing," Hendricks said. "I was out cold. When I came to, the first thing I saw was Gotay, standing over me, shaking his finger, saying, 'I told you it was bad luck.'"

Did the experience convince Hendricks to respect the power of chicken-bone crosses? Hardly.

"I told Julio, 'Get the hell out of here,'" Hendricks said. "I told him, 'That doesn't have a damn thing to do with me getting hit.'"

Gotay wandered off, shaking his head and muttering to himself, more resolute than ever about keeping a safe distance from crosses.

Mark Kotsay and Jason Kendall

On the first day of spring training in 2005, Oakland Athletics outfielder Mark Kotsay opened a clear plastic bag containing cigars and carefully placed them in a personal humidor in his clubhouse locker. Kotsay's new teammate, Jason Kendall, could not believe his eyes. He, too, is a cigar smoker.

The two don't wait until after an expensive meal to indulge themselves with a fine cigar and perhaps a smooth cognac. Both will light up at the ballpark. Kendall, a three-time All-Star catcher who was traded from the Pittsburgh Pirates, will smoke a cigar, or at least take a couple of draws, before a game.

Kotsay, on occasion, will retreat to the clubhouse during a game and fire up a stogie while he waits for his turn at-bat. "You're kidding?" Kendall said. "During a game? I've never done that."

Kotsay's eyes lit up. "I wasn't hitting worth a damn," he said, "and one day decided to give it a try. You know what happened? I went deep twice in that game. I've been doing it ever since."

Has anyone taken issue with Kotsay for smoking during a game?

"Uh, yeah, Billy Beane," Kotsay said, referring to the A's general manager. "One time he was in the clubhouse during a game, and I was smoking a cigar. He said, 'What the hell are you doing?' I told him my story, about hitting the two homers."

Beane's response?

"He told me, 'Next time, take those sons of bitches to the plate with you,'" Kotsay said.

Ray Miller

Since the day he first got to the major leagues in 1978 as the Baltimore Orioles pitching coach, Ray Miller has made certain to sit in the exact same location in the dugout, no matter what ballpark he is in. That would seem to be a superstitious practice, although Miller claims he has a practical reason for his choice of vantage points: It allows him a consistent look and angle from which to evaluate his pitchers' performances.

RESERVED FO

"Whatever," says Scott McGregor, one of seven different pitchers who has been a 20-game winner on Miller's watch. "Ray had the most superstitious stuff," said McGregor, who pitched for the Orioles from 1976 to 1988.

"He would take the exact number of steps running from the foul line to the dugout every time. As soon as he hit the dugout steps, he would snap his fingers on one hand into his other hand, and then he would run and sit down."

Miller would faithfully tap his knuckles on the dugout bench for good luck, as well.

"He had all kinds of stuff going on," McGregor said. "I'd look over at him and say, 'Are we ready now?' He'd say, 'Yeah, we're ready now.'"

Miller began his third term as the Orioles pitching coach in 2004. He also was the Pittsburgh Pirates pitching coach for 10 years, and the manager of the Minnesota Twins for two years in the mid-1980s and of the Orioles for two years in the late 1990s. He has been around long enough to understand that superstitious behavior in baseball players is a coping mechanism.

"It's solace," Miller said. "It's about, If I do this, things will be good, so it's a positive thought. You can get carried away with it, though, and go too far."

Rich Donnelly

Milwaukee Brewers third base coach Rich Donnelly doesn't consider himself to be superstitious. After all, he's been stepping on cracks for years.

"I read a lot about superstitions when I was younger, and I just didn't believe any of it," said Donnelly, who began his 23rd season as a Major League Baseball coach in 2005. "One day I just starting walking around looking for cracks to step on. I stepped on every one." And he's been doing it ever since.

Donnelly might be the only person in the major leagues who intentionally steps on the foul lines. Most will go into a gymnastics routine to avoid touching the white chalk line when entering and leaving the playing field.

Superstitious though he claims he's not, Donnelly always has a wad of chewing gum in his mouth when he's in the coach's box, and he moves the gum around according to the situation. If a runner is on second base, he will shift his gum to the left side of his mouth. If no one is on second, he keeps the gum in his right cheek. "There have been lots of mornings when I woke up with a sore right side of the mouth," he joked.

Donnelly spent 14 years on former manager Jim Leyland's coaching staff with the Pittsburgh Pirates, Florida Marlins and Colorado Rockies. During the Marlins' run to the 1997 World Series title, Donnelly wore the same T-shirt under his uniform jersey for every postseason game. It was a Steubenville (Ohio) High School football shirt—one of his sons played on the team.

"I had to wear my Big Red football shirt every single game," Donnelly said. "I couldn't go out there without it. That was my gamer."

No one in the Marlins clubhouse considered it unusual behavior for a middle-aged man to wear the same shirt every day for several weeks. Heck, most everyone in the room had their own idiosyncrasies.

"Ballplayers are like trained animals," Donnelly said. "They come to the ballpark, and everything has to be the same. They don't like anything that knocks them off their routine.

"Just look at the dugout; you'll see every guy sitting in the same spot every night. If a guy comes up from the minors and sits here, they'll say, 'Hey, Jim sits here; find another seat.'"

> "There have been lots of mornings when I woke up with a sore right side of the mouth."

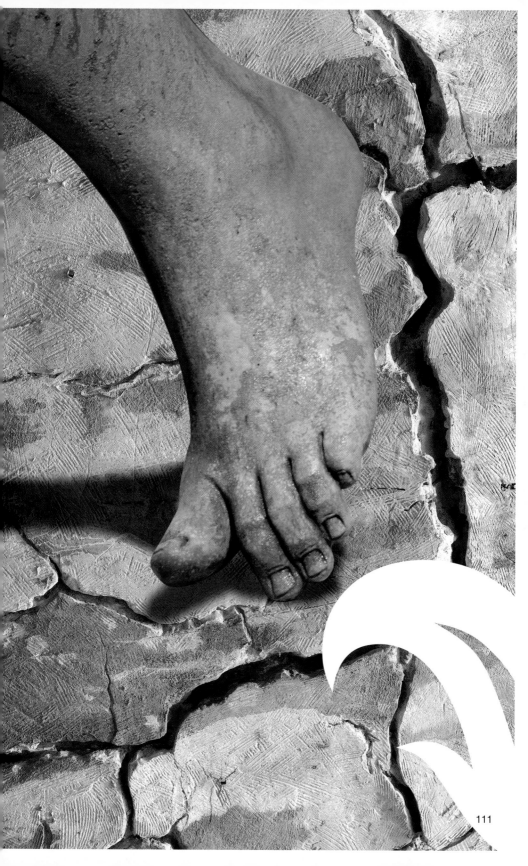

Billy Beane

Billy Beane, general manager of the Oakland Athletics, is a bright and innovative executive who has kept his small-market team highly competitive in an industry of widely disparate operating budgets. His genius and methods are laid out in the bestselling book *Moneyball*.

Yet for someone who relies more on statistical geeks and college professors than on hunch-playing managers and sun-crusted scouts when putting together his team's roster, Beane falls into the traditional baseball norm from at least one perspective: He's just as superstitious as the next guy.

"It's not because this stuff works—I'm not that irrational," Beane said. "It's just because it keeps me sane."

What keeps him sane varies. "Some things work at home; some things work on the road," he said.

When Beane isn't with the A's on the road, he often watches their games on television, while working out in the team's weight training room. Well, part of the game. When the A's aren't batting, he's pushing buttons on the remote control.

"I watch another game," Beane said. "And I make sure I don't look when they flash the scores on the screen. I try to guess when our lineup is coming to bat, and I switch the channel back to our game then."

Why does he only watch the A's when they are batting? "If I'm just watching our offense," Beane said, "we can't fall behind while I'm watching."

However, if Beane feels confident that the A's have the edge in the pitching matchup—Barry Zito, Tim Hudson and Mark Mulder provided plenty of those situations in recent years—he reverses his pattern. If Beane chooses to watch the A's pitcher, as soon as the side is retired, he switches channels to another game while the A's take their turn at-bat. "When I turn it back and we've scored four runs, I get an incredible rush," he said.

Beane is every bit as superstitious when the A's are playing at home. Say they have a one- or two-run lead in the seventh inning. Under those circumstances, Beane often will head out to his car, tune in the San Francisco Giants game on the radio, and start driving home. The trip takes 35 to 40 minutes.

"I'll pick a spot on the way, say two-thirds of the way, and when I get to that point, I'll turn back to our station, and all I want to hear is [announcer] Bill King's voice wrapping it up," Beane said. "Because if he's wrapping it up, then I know we've won."

If the game is not over, Beane is crestfallen, because Oakland's opponent has likely tied the score or got ahead.

Sometimes Beane will live dangerously and depart for home with the score tied. He'll never forget the time he did that, and just as he switched from the Giants game to the A's, Jeremy Giambi cracked a game-winning home run.

"One time it worked against me," Beane said. Did it ever. He was driving home on June 1, 2004, and had yet to tune in the A's game when his cell phone rang. It was David Forst, the team's assistant general manager. "They took him to the hospital," Forst said somberly. "They think he broke his hand."

Beane, of course, had no idea what Forst was talking about. Third baseman Eric Chavez, the A's best player, had been hit with a pitch. He suffered a broken right hand and was out for five weeks.

Beane was listening when the A's won the game in the 12th inning on Bobby Kielty's home run, but his night had been ruined. "I wasn't even happy," Beane said.

Jeff Hamilton

When they were teammates on the Los Angeles Dodgers from 1988 to 1990, catcher Rick Dempsey would often stop on his drive to the ballpark to pick up third baseman Jeff Hamilton. Dempsey probably would have done it if he had to go far out of his way, just for the amusement value.

Hamilton would walk out of his house, stop abruptly, turn around and go back in. He would repeat that sequence twice more before continuing on to Dempsey's awaiting car. And Hamilton would get into the car only after he had spit three times.

"Everything was in multiples of three with Jeff," said Mickey Hatcher, a Dodgers outfielder of that era. "He would take the field, and during warm-ups he would throw three rocks off the field. He would spit three times.

"When he came into the dugout, he would lay his glove on the bench and pick it up three times. He'd lay it down, lay it down, lay it down, and then finally close it and leave it alone."

When Hamilton waited in the on-deck circle, he rubbed his bat with pine tar three times. Before settling into the batter's box, he took three practice swings and some-

times six, but never two or four.

His uniform number was 33. On team rosters, he was listed at 6-foot-3 and 207 pounds—multiples of three. He was born in March, the third month. And, of course, Hamilton played third base.

If only he could have batted .300. Hamilton never came close. In six major league seasons, 1986 to 1991, all with the Dodgers, he batted .234 with 24 home runs and 124 RBI. He was a regular on the 1988 World Series championship team, the most recent Dodgers team to accomplish that feat.

While Hamilton didn't have a distinguished career, his contemporaries won't soon forget him.

"He had thousands of things he did with three," Hatcher said. "It was unbelievable. I've never seen anything like it."

Manny Ramirez

Boston Red Sox left fielder Manny Ramirez is among the most feared hitters of his generation—and one of the most pleasant smelling, too.

Entering 2005, Ramirez had a .316 batting average and 390 home runs in his 12 major league seasons, along with a trophy for being selected the Most Valuable Player of the 2004 World Series, an event that the Red Sox won for the first time in 86 years. The scent of success indeed is sweet.

"When I was there," said longtime relief pitcher Todd Jones, who spent two months in 2003 with the Red Sox, "Manny had this real expensive bottle of cologne, probably cost $300. He would shower after batting practice and get ready for the game. Right before going out to the field, he would spray a couple of hits of cologne on his neck.

"Then he'd go out and do his thing, maybe hit two or three homers."

That probably had more to do with Ramirez's ability to hit a baseball than to whether he smelled of Brut, Polo, Jack Daniel's, Mountain Dew or sweaty socks. Nevertheless, his teammates clamored for a splash of Manny's lucky cologne.

"Pretty soon, guys were like, 'Spray me! Spray me!'" Jones said. "Guys were lining up at Manny's locker to get good luck sprays. Manny loved it."

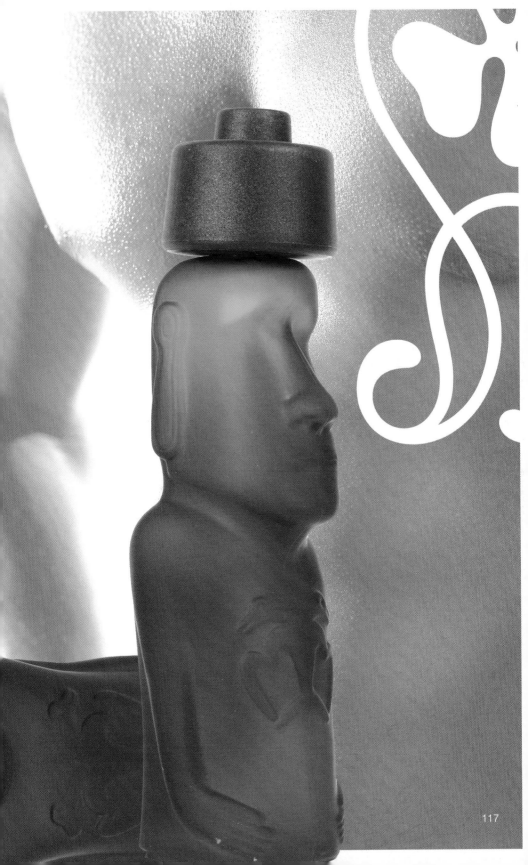

Mike Cuellar

Mike Cuellar didn't become a star in the major leagues until he was 32. By that time, he was engaged in more superstitious practices and rituals than you could shake a voodoo stick at. Cuellar afforded the Baltimore Orioles of the early 1970s not only formidable pitching, but also a constant source of entertainment.

Cuellar always wore blue on the day he pitched. His pants, shirt, tie, socks, jacket, underwear and shoes were some shade of his lucky color. As his success grew and his paychecks got bigger, Cuellar bought a sky blue Cadillac to drive to the ballpark.

Once he stepped over the foul line—never on it—and headed for the pitcher's mound, Cuellar expected one of the infielders to hand him the ball to start the inning. "If they forgot and tossed it to him," said Frank Robinson, a Hall of Fame outfielder on those Orioles teams, "he'd step back and let it go by. The ball had to be handed to him."

When he retired a batter, Cuellar would accept a throw after the ball had been tossed around the infield—but only from the third baseman. If the shortstop had the ball, Cuellar would wave off his throw, and the shortstop would have to get the attention of the third baseman.

Climbing atop the mound was no mindless task for Cuellar, either.

"He always walked around the mound and approached it from the front," Robinson said. "Didn't matter where he was. If he was in the back of the mound, he'd walk on the grass all the way around it until he was at the front, and then approach that way."

Back in the dugout when it was the Orioles' turn to bat, Cuellar would head for the tunnel leading to the clubhouse and light a cigarette. "As soon as the first out was made, he'd put it out," said Elrod Hendricks, an Orioles catcher of that period. "Maybe he only had one drag sometimes, but he'd still put it out. That was his superstition."

Cuellar and Hendricks shared a hotel room when the Orioles were on the road. Before going to bed at night, Cuellar closed and locked the windows, and stuffed paper under the door and in the keyhole. "To keep the evil spirits out," Hendricks said.

Even then, Cuellar wasn't comfortable. He insisted on keeping a light on throughout the night. "To ward off the ghosts," Hendricks said. The roommates reached a compromise. They slept with the bathroom light on.

Cuellar wore the same Orioles cap for an entire season. Even in its deteriorated condition, it remained his good luck cap and he was loath to pitch without it. On one occasion, the team was in Chicago and Cuellar's cap was in Baltimore. "We were in a pennant race, near the end of the year," said longtime Orioles pitching coach Ray Miller, "and Mike was telling us seriously he couldn't pitch without his hat."

A call was placed to Baltimore, and a team employee was soon on an airplane to deliver Cuellar's cap. Oops. Wrong cap. "Turned out there were several caps in his locker, and the kid didn't bring them all," Miller said. Cuellar reluctantly pitched that night, but he lost.

What became of the cap carrier? "Probably the kid got fired," Miller said.

The Orioles gladly indulged Cuellar's eccentricities and idiosyncrasies. He was money in the bank from 1969 to 1974, winning 125 games against 63 losses in that six-year period, four times achieving at least 20 victories. By then he was getting old, and Cuellar's inconsistent performance over the next two seasons provided Orioles manager Earl Weaver with his most famous quotation: "I gave Cuellar more chances than I gave my first wife."

The Orioles released Cuellar in 1976. Presumably he drove away in a blue automobile.

Jim Leyland

All those years managing in the minor leagues primed Jim Leyland to become one of the best major league managers during his run with the Pittsburgh Pirates, Florida Marlins and Colorado Rockies from 1986 to 1999. It also helped him develop a couple of habits that he swore helped his teams win games.

The first: "If we'd win, I'd write the lineup out the next day with the same pen," Leyland said. "If I couldn't find it, I'd go crazy."

Leyland's pen habit became so obsessive that it didn't take long for his coaching staff to pick up on it. "And then sometimes my coaches would hide it," Leyland said. "Different guys would take it. Rich Donnelly or Tommy Sandt would take my pen, or magic marker, whatever I used, and they'd put it in their pocket. Just to drive me crazy."

Everyone knows you don't mess with superstitions: The coaches might have amused themselves by confiscating Leyland's lucky pens and watching his agitated reaction, but they always returned them in time for the manager to use for posting the lineup.

Leyland religiously clung to one other superstitious habit throughout his major league career. Remember all those television shots revealing him nervously sneaking a drag off a cigarette in the tunnel off the dugout? "I'd always put my cigarette out with two outs in the ninth inning if we were winning," Leyland said.

If his teams were losing, it didn't much matter. He would puff away—always back in the tunnel. Baseball rules prohibit smoking in the dugout.

If his teams were winning, like clockwork, with two outs, Leyland would smash out his butt in anticipation of taking another victory into the clubhouse with him. "I don't know how it started," he said. "It was a minor league thing."

Leo Mazzone

The sight of Atlanta Braves pitching coach Leo Mazzone seated next to manager Bobby Cox in the dugout, rocking back and forth, is a television staple. Mazzone says he has done that since he was young, and it has nothing to do with superstition.

Mazzone, however, is an ardent Notre Dame fan and will almost always wear a Notre Dame T-shirt under his Braves jersey. The exception, Mazzone says, is when he wears a T-shirt bearing the name of his son's baseball team.

Mazzone said he can leave his condominium and take either a right or a left turn and get to Atlanta's Turner Field in the same amount of time. If Mazzone takes a right and the Braves win, he will take a right the next day. Otherwise, he is inclined to turn left.

At Turner Field, Mazzone sits on the bench precisely where two padded areas join, putting him over a small opening in the upholstery. Typically, he's centered over that opening, but Mazzone, who preaches the importance of throwing the down-and-away strike, will move to his left if the Braves pitcher needs a down-and-away strike to a left-handed hitter, and to his right if that pitch is needed against a right-handed hitter.

Kevin Rhomberg

Touchy-feely **had a unique meaning for Kevin Rhomberg, an outfielder who played in 41 games for the Cleveland Indians from 1982 to 1984. Rhomberg refused to be touched last. That's right, if someone touched him, he had to touch that person back.**

It made for some humorous situations. Rhomberg would be in the batter's box when the catcher would reach out and touch him. Before readying himself for the next pitch, Rhomberg had to touch the catcher.

While at bat, Rhomberg usually did not have to go far to get the last touch. But on the bases, it was a different matter.

Minnesota Twins manager Ron Gardenhire, a former infielder, played against Rhomberg in the minor leagues. Gardenhire said that when Rhomberg was on second base, infielders would sidle over, touch him and scoot away. To return the touch would mean wandering off second base, and Rhomberg, less bothered by how it looked than how it felt, would do just that.

Craig Biggio

Ten years ago, Craig Biggio would have declined to discuss anything having to do with superstitions. He would have vehemently denied that he was remotely superstitious, insisted that none of his quirky habits had anything to do with superstition and then hid in a corner hoping the baseball gods had not heard him.

The baseball gods are a powerful force in Biggio's professional life. Upset them, and Biggio would have to say goodbye to any good fortune he might be experiencing.

> ## "If you put the doughnut down in one spot, and you get a hit, you try to put it down in the same spot next time."

But Biggio is older now, a 17-year veteran of the major leagues entering the 2005 season, all with the Houston Astros. He claims he has mellowed and is not nearly as nutty as he once was, back in the day when he believed that how often he changed his lucky underwear had as much to do with hitting and winning as what he did with a fastball in his happy zone.

Biggio says he no longer sacrifices personal hygiene for the sake of a hitting streak. His locker isn't the sweetest-smelling domain in the clubhouse, but not for a lack of effort. Wear the same underwear without washing it for two weeks? "That's kind of nasty—not for me," he said.

Biggio still lets pine tar build into a slimy mess atop his batting helmet, and he will throw away his batting gloves if he has a few bad games. But his biggest quirk these days? "I think I have a doughnut issue," he said.

When he is in the on-deck circle, Biggio takes a few swings with a weighted doughnut on his bat. What he does with the doughnut when he removes it from his bat depends on how he's hitting. Sometimes he flips it to the teammate batting behind him. Sometimes he bangs it on the ground.

"If you put the doughnut down in one spot, and you get a hit, you try to put it down in the same spot next time," he said. "And you'll probably get another hit."

When Biggio was the Astros' leadoff batter, he flipped the doughnut to No. 2 batter Adam Everett. The two switched places in the batting order in 2005. No. 3 hitter Jeff Bagwell doesn't use a doughnut on the on-deck circle. "So I can't flip it to him," Biggio said. "Now I'm on my own."

Why do baseball players seem to be more superstitious than other athletes? "Simple," Biggio said: "Baseball is the only sport in which players do not control the ball. So in addition to skill, luck is involved."

"Guys throw a round object at you, and you have to hit it," Biggio said. "Hockey players control the puck. In basketball, you shoot a ball. In baseball, you can hit the ball great, but you might hit it right at a guy. You have to be lucky. I've always said I'd rather be lucky than good."

Biggio might change his batting gloves every once in a while or chuck his bat if he's in a slump, but he is acutely aware that his equipment has little to do with his performance.

"We like to say: 'It's never the Indian; it's always the bow and arrow,'" Biggio said. "In reality we know the truth: It's the Indian. But every once in a while, you change the bow and arrow, and it works."

Roger Clemens

During a pregame ceremony in April 2005 honoring Roger Clemens for his seventh Cy Young Award, his Houston Astros teammates offered congratulations in a video tribute played on the stadium JumboTron. "He's the only guy who has more Cy Young's than children," marveled one guy.

Roger and Debbie Clemens have four sons. Had they decided to have a child for each Cy Young Award he won, they would have seven children whose given names start with the letter K.

K is the baseball scoring code for strikeout, and Roger in his 21-year career had struck out more batters than anyone else in major league history, except Nolan Ryan, entering the 2005 season.

In 1986, soon after Roger became the first major league player to strike out 20 batters in a game, Debbie gave birth to their first son. She liked the name Coby,

a variation of Jacob. "Instead of *C*, we said, let's put a *K* on it," Roger said.

Three more sons arrived over the next decade, and the Clemenses stuck with the K trend. Kory was second, followed by Kacy, who got his name partly because of the last two letters—c and y—as in Cy, of Cy Young. Last came Kody, whose midde name is Alek, not Alec or Alex.

Koby, Kory, Kacy, Kody—any hopes for a Kay, a Kelly, or a Katy? "We had a few girls names in mind," Roger said, "but we didn't get anything with long hair. We tried."

"Instead of **C**, we said, let's put a **K** on it."